The Ghost o

Ma

A continuation of the biography *The Ghost of White Hart Lane* by Rob White and Julie Welch

Best wishes
Rob

methuen | drama
LONDON • NEW YORK • OXFORD • NEW DELHI • SYDNEY

METHUEN DRAMA
Bloomsbury Publishing Plc
50 Bedford Square, London, WC1B 3DP, UK
1385 Broadway, New York, NY 10018, USA
29 Earlsfort Terrace, Dublin 2, Ireland

BLOOMSBURY, METHUEN DRAMA and the Methuen
Drama logo are trademarks of Bloomsbury Publishing Plc

First published in Great Britain 2024

A catalogue record for this book is available from the British Library.

A catalog record for this book is available from the Library of Congress.

ISBN: PB: 978-1-3505-2244-2
ePDF: 978-1-3505-2245-9
eBook: 978-1-3505-2246-6

Series: Modern Plays

Typeset by Mark Heslington Ltd, Scarborough, North Yorkshire
Printed and bound in Great Britain

To find out more about our authors and books visit
www.bloomsbury.com and sign up for our newsletters.

Writer/Director – Martin Murphy

Martin is a writer, director, performer and workshop leader. His recent writing credits include *Midas* (2023) and *Jonny Feathers the Rock & Roll Pigeon* (2022), both at Park Theatre. Martin's previous writing credits include *Jury* (Park Theatre/Zoom), *Victim* (Pleasance Courtyard/King's Head Theatre), *Worlds* (VAULT Festival), *Rockstar* (Lyric Hammersmith), *Villain* (Soho Theatre/Underbelly) and *Manor* (Soho Theatre). *Villain* and *Victim* are both published by Methuen Drama.

Martin also directed *Villain*, *Worlds* and *Victim*. As a workshop leader Martin works for the National Theatre working with teenage playwrights all over the country as part of their New Views competition. As a performer Martin was half of musical comedy double act Pistol & Jack who played at over a hundred venues across the UK and internationally including Secret Garden Party, Assembly Edinburgh, NuWrite Festival (Zagreb), Madame Jojos's and Soho Theatre.

Associate Director – Bronagh Lagan

Originally from Northern Ireland, Bronagh is an award-winning director passionate about directing new writing, particularly from underrepresented communities.

Bronagh's Olivier Award-nominated production of *Cruise* by Jack Holden was the first new play to open the West End after the pandemic.

Most recently Bronagh directed *Flowers for Mrs Harris* starring Jenna Russell which featured as one of *The Stage*'s Top 50 productions of 2023 and won a What's On Stage Award for Best Off-West End Production. She also directed the UK regional tour of *The Rise and Fall of Little Voice* starring Christina Bianco.

Bronagh's production of *Rags*, the musical by Charles Strouse and Stephen Schwartz, received nine Off West End Theatre Award nominations, including Best Director and Best Production. She worked closely with Stephen Schwartz in reimagining the script for an actor-musician production and curated a cast album. She also directed the European premiere of *Little Women*, the musical at the Park Theatre which is available on Broadway HD.

Bronagh directed the premieres of original musicals *Broken Wings* (Haymarket) and *Rumi* (ENO) and the bilingual biopic *Umm Kulthum*, all of which have toured the Middle East including the prestigious Dubai Opera House and National Theatre of Bahrain.

Executive Producer – Rob White

Rob White is a photographer and writer. He has been a commercial photographer for most of his career specialising in food and still life. In 2011 Rob, along with Julie Welch, co-authored a biography of his late father, the Tottenham and Scotland legend John White. Rob was just five months when his dad was tragically killed, at the age of twenty-seven, after being struck by lightning whilst playing golf at Crews Hill golf course. The critically acclaimed book *The Ghost of White Hart Lane* (2011) details Rob's search for the father that he never knew. It not only tells the story of a brilliantly gifted footballer, but also of a lost era.

In 2024 Rob commissioned Martin Murphy to write the play as a way of marking the sixtieth anniversary of his dad's death. The world premiere was held at the Tottenham Hotspur Stadium on 21 July 2024, which was the exact date sixty years on of the fatal accident.

Rob is a self-confessed football addict who now lives within the shadow of the Tottenham Hotspur Stadium, North London.

Performer – Cal Newman

Cal Newman is an actor, writer and director from Gloucestershire having trained at the Manchester School of Theatre and with the National Youth Theatre. His most recent credits include appearing in *Londres* at Park Theatre in 2023. He also wrote, directed, produced and featured in an original play titled *Where We Are Now* which debuted at the Old Red Lion Theatre in 2022 before being revived for a limited time at Annka Kultys Gallery the following year. Cal has also been featured in NYT's *The Story of Our Youth* at Shaftesbury Theatre as well as a touring production of *To Sir, with Love* with the Touring Consortium.

Production Manager and Lighting and Sound Design – Amée Smith

Amée Smith works regularly as a production manager and producer while keeping up with the on-stage life of many a show as a stage manager and technical stage manager.

With a background in theatre, comedy and immersive work as both a performer and producer, Amée is also an experienced arts publicist giving her a well-rounded view of the running of any performance as a whole.

She first worked with Bruised Sky in 2017 and has been involved with multiple Bruised Sky productions since then both in London and at Edinburgh Festival Fringe.

Set and Video Design – Matt Powell

Matt (they/she/he) is a non-binary, Offie finalist video designer, musical theatre creative and queer practitioner based in the East Midlands. They are a part-time PhD candidate exploring LGBTQ+ representation in musical theatre at the University of Wolverhampton.

Video design and digital credits include: *New Year* (Birmingham Opera Company); *Marie Curie* (Charing Cross

Theatre); *RENT* (May Hall); *Laughing Boy* (Jermyn Street Theatre); *Ride* (The Old Globe, San Diego, Curve, Southwark Playhouse); *Sherlock and the Poison Wood* (Watermill Theatre); *Exhibitionists* (King's Head Theatre); *I Really Do Think That This Will Change Your Life* (Stage Awards for Innovation Nominee – Mercury Theatre, Colchester); *Rebecca* (Charing Cross Theatre); *Animal* (Offie finalist for Video Design – Hope Mill Theatre/Park Theatre); *Accidental Death of an Anarchist* (Theatre Royal Haymarket, Sheffield Theatres, Lyric Hammersmith); *Rumi: The Musical* (D'asha Performing Arts Festival, London Coliseum); *How a City Can Save the World* (Sheffield Theatres); *A-Typical Rainbow* (Turbine Theatre); *Flight* (Royal College of Music); *But What If You Die* (Camden People's Theatre); *Old Friends* (digital); *Bloody Difficult Women* (Riverside Studios); *Santa Must Die* (Alphabetti Theatre); *Snowflake* (The Lowry); *34* (Aria Entertainment/The Lowry); *Public Domain* (Vaudeville Theatre/Southwark Playhouse); *On Hope: A Digital Song Cycle* (The Other Palace).

Recent directing credits include: *RENT* (May Hall); *Santa Must Die* (Leeds Playhouse/Red Ladder); *Nativity: The Musical* (Derby Theatre); *The Unconventionals* (VAULT Festival); *Crazy for You* (Derby Theatre); *Is He Musical?* (Curve, The Other Palace)

www.matt-powell.co.uk | @mattpowellcreative

Producer – Ellie Stone

Ellie Stone is a freelance theatre producer. Credits for Bruised Sky Productions include *Thirsty* by Stephanie Martin, *4* by Sarah Milton, *Batman and the Queen* by David Scinto, *Vivarium* by Don Mc Camphill and *Victim* by Martin Murphy. She is also Creative Producer for the charity Action for Children's Arts.

Producer – Stuart Croll

Stuart Croll is a producer, writer and event manager. He has produced several feature films, short films, theatrical events and stage plays, and has written comedy for television and radio programmes as well as for the stage in London and at the Edinburgh Festival.

Stuart is also an author, journalist and editor, having worked for a host of national newspapers, magazines, radio shows, television and websites.

(And he is related to Spurs' double-winning goalkeeper Bill Brown.)

Graphic and Content Design and Support – Colin Goodwin

Colin Goodwin works primarily in the digital sphere, creating engaging online content and graphics. As Content and Brand Coordinator at the Royal College of Paediatrics and Child Health, he actively seeks to work on projects that help build a better understanding and society. He has worked on several projects with Bruised Sky.

Cover Design – Futbolista

Mark Sydor, founder of Futbolista: Futbolista combines my lifelong passion for art, design and the beautiful game. As a Tottenham Hotspur supporter, whose work leans heavily on nostalgia, it's an honour to be involved in a project that celebrates the life of one of the greatest players in our history.

Bruised Sky Productions

Bruised Sky Productions was founded by James Kermack in 2009 with Executive Director Martin Murphy joining the company later that year. Based in N17 North London the aim of Bruised Sky is to produce brutal, funny and brave new writing, with no apologies and no excuses.

They have produced shows at Park Theatre, Soho Theatre, VAULT Festival and both Edinburgh and Dublin fringe festivals. During lockdown they produced Bruised Sky-Solation, an online project working with over thirty artists which received over 100,000 views.

Special thanks to Julie Welch, James Kermack, Callan McCarthy, Julia Murray, Carol Murphy, Andrew Murray, David Knowles, Tony Stevens, Tottenham Hotspur FC, Park Theatre, Amelia Cherry, Daniel Goldman, Nikki Adams, Huw Roberts, John Wynne, David Rees, Knut Henriksen, Pete Spara, Heikki Henriksen, Carey Davis, Hannah Murphy, Jeremy Somerscales, Linda Baker, Ralph Dixon, Cliff Jones, Kevin Millband, Steve Perryman, Neil Humphries, Justin Sanderson.

Martin Murphy's note

In autumn 2023 Rob White got in touch and said he wanted me to write a play to mark the sixtieth anniversary of his dad's death. My family are huge Spurs fans going back three generations and I grew up knowing the story of John White so this was a fantastic honour, but with that came a huge responsibility. I had to get this right.

Research-wise I was already familiar with Rob and the great Julie Welch's book. I combined this with some fun weeks combing through old highlights of games from the Sixties, internet articles and of course long chats with Rob.

The task was then to try and edit an entire lifetime into a sixty-minute play. Once this was in decent enough shape we held a rehearsed reading of the play at Park Theatre which a representative from Spurs attended. The outcome of this was Spurs offered to host the premiere of *The Ghost of White Hart Lane* on 21 July 2024, sixty years to the day of John White's death.

Having a play at the Tottenham Hotspur Stadium is an absolute dream come true for me and I can't wait to share this extraordinary story with the world.

The Ghost of White Hart Lane

Characters

John White, *twenty-seven years old when we meet him. Scottish, cheeky, footballer.*

Rob White, *John White's son. A young boy we watch grow.*

Setting

From Musselburgh to Tottenham we move back and forward from the 1940s to the present day.

Notes

The play can be performed as a one-person show with a single performer playing father, son and various characters we meet along the journey.

Punctuation and spelling are used to indicate delivery, not to conform to the rules of grammar.

Pre-show

As audience enter the space the stage is bare other than a single box placed centre stage. A single beam highlights this box as it sits there closed.

Scene One

21 July 1964. **John White** *is centre stage in full Spurs kit knelt posing with a brown leather football. He smiles at us, a mischievous glint in his eye.*

FLASH.

A sudden flash of light temporarily blinds us but this is gone just as fast. We are left in the black, then snap, we realise the flash was that of a photographer's light as an image fills the stage – it is that of the 1964/65 Spurs team.

The image slowly fades as we go back to black for a moment before **John White**'s *return lights up the room for us again.*

John *now stands centre stage in just his pants.*

John   I do believe that cheeky Welsh swine Cliff Jones has stolen my trousers. This is the start, pre-season training, team photo, only first eleven invited in today. Couple of the lads feeling a bit left out, those not been asked in today. You're not in the photo then you're not in the manager's plans.

I'm there. Bill Nicholson has said he's building his new team around me. That's his decision, like a thousand little ones we make every day and his choice to build a team around me is based on a thousand tiny decisions I make. On the pitch, on the training ground, in life. Jimmy Greaves up front sums this up better than anyone. 'It's not about being in the right place at the right time, it's about being in the right place all the time.'

Photos taken, light training session, running, they call that a run? I've not got started and we're being called back in.

'Well done today, boys, bright and early tomorrow, yeah?'
Not Bill Nick's voice, anyone he ever gave a well done to, he
made it clear, that a pat on the back is only a few inches away
from a kick up the arse. Not Harry's voice, no we'll not hear
Harry's voice again. Cecil Poynton, he sends us back in to
get changed but I'm not done yet.

See if I head back in there then this is a very different story.
What happens to me that day, ten million to one, ten million
tiny different decisions I could have made in the twenty-
seven years I've been alive which means this story doesn't
end up the way it does. That ten million to one lightning
strike doesn't hit, leaving my wife a widow and my kids
growing up without a dad. But I'm not done training for the
day, not even close.

I see Terry Medwin, he's recovering from injury and needs a
bit more exercise to get him up to speed, Bill Nick hands me
two rackets. 'You get that bastard working up a sweat.' I nod.
'Knock some balls around, Terry?' Terry looks me up and
down in just my pants. 'I can take them off if you like?' 'No
you're alright, John.' He grabs a racket and we play against
the wall.

He starts playing squash.

I'm battering Terry, got him running all over the place, I've
barely broken a sweat and he's slipping over in a pile of his. I
keep moving him round the gym. Cliff Jones walks by.
'Game of golf after this, Cliff?' 'It's gonna piss down, John.'
'Aye more like you're pissing yourself worried I'll wipe the
floor with you again.' Cliff laughs and goes, but not straight
out, goes by where our clothes are in the dressing room. I
figure he must have left something. While my mind's
distracted Terry gets a shot away and . . . 'Fine, I'll give you
that one. I'm off for a round of golf.'

Scene Two

1972. North London. **Rob White**, *eight years old sneaks on to the stage. He puts a finger to his lips to indicate we should 'shh' as what he is doing is clearly a secret.*

Rob *searches for something and then spots it, a box, covered in dust. He picks the box up and shows it to us proudly.*

Rob   My dad's in this box. Not my actual dad obviously, his stuff's all in here though. My name's Rob White. I'm eight years old, my favourite food is fish fingers and my favourite colour is aqua. My dad's . . . well, you know who my dad was, everyone knows my dad except me. All I know is he's in here. My dad's in this box in the attic. Mum keeps him up there. So I don't ask about him, I'm a good boy, I don't want to make my mum cry.

He puts the box down and is about to open it then looks a little unsure.

See I know she keeps this up here, shut away. We don't have pictures of Dad downstairs. People look at me and they say 'Oh he looks just like him' then they sadly look away. We don't have pictures of my dad around the house. But I want to know, do I look like my dad? What was he like? What did he sound like? What made him laugh? I'm a big boy now, I'm big enough to know these things. But I don't want to make my mum cry.

These last words fall heavily on young **Rob** *and he decides to put the box back.*

I don't want to make mum cry.

He puts the box back but in doing so he knocks over a case. He picks the case up and reads some initials.

J.A.W. John Anderson White. My dad.

A sudden rush overtakes young **Rob** *and he cannot resist opening the box. He pulls out an old pair of football boots, he stares at them in awe.*

My dad's in this box. My dad the football legend.

He opens the box, we hear the clatter of studs, as lights fade.

Scene Three

1945. Musselburgh. **John White**, *eight years old, is holding a tennis ball.*

John   Keepie up. It's what I do all the time. See football's a team game, need a group of you, but football is all I want to do. So keepy up well you don't need a team for that you don't even need two of you. You don't even need a football. Tennis ball, golf ball, an old orange. Tom and Eddie can't get it off me, they try but I just keep going. Left foot, half an hour I keep it in the air, right foot, another half an hour.

Tom and Eddie are out in the yard. 'Pass us it' they say. I laugh. 'Come get it off me then' I say, they try but I'm too quick for either of them. So they try to knock me off the ball, they're strong boys my brothers but I'm strong too. From birth I've had it, he's too small, too weak, he won't survive.

I'm born too early and they have to feed me through an eye dropper I'm so small, they send Eddie away for a year so Mum can focus on me, help me grow and I do. So now I'm strong, I'm quick, way too fast for my brothers trying to get this ball off me, I see them coming but they don't see me go, like a ghost I'm gone and so's the ball. And they're getting right annoyed with me now and they go inside, it's gone quiet like they've given up.

I hear them giggling by the window upstairs, they're laughing but I know what they're gonna do. Window opens above me and out they pour a bucket of water trying to drench me, but I'm too quick for that too. See every tiny decision you make in life can make a difference. I move and that bucket of water leaves a big puddle on the floor in our yard, I'm too quick for them. Where you are to that exact second can make all the difference.

See if the ball's in the air that's all I need to focus on. So they can't get it off me, that ball's still in the air and they can shout at me, try to knock me but I'm keeping it up in the air, nothing's going to stop me until my ma's voice. 'John come inside, it's your dad. Your dad's dead.' And the darkness starts, days get shorter, darkness gets longer.

Scene Four

May 1973. North London. We watch footage of the build-up to the 1973 FA Cup Final between Sunderland and Leeds. **Rob White**, *nine years old, watches the build-up excitedly.*

Rob   It's FA Cup Final day, which means football on all morning. This is the one day of the year when you can actually watch football live on TV. (*Huge excitement.*) BBC and ITV, it's amazing. Both channels competing, like the teams, but battling with each other for viewers. And to kick off the day ITV. It's a *cup final* knockout. I'm watching and I'm re-enacting everything around our living room climbing on the sofas and Mum's telling me she's going to turn it off if I don't stop then something else comes on.

It's highlights, they're replaying action from previous finals and suddenly there he is. My dad. I'd never seen him moving before. There he is alive in front of me. Not alive obviously, not even in colour. We've a colour TV, but Dad's in black and white, this is from history. But brought back to life there in front of me on screen and my whole world changes.

This feels like a premonition come true, before that moment I had no idea that footage of my dad even existed but there he is, this man in the number 8 shirt, a man I've never seen before but I just know, that's my dad. Not a sad memory we never talk about. Not a ghost we keep locked in a box upstairs, he's there, my dad, I can see him. Lifting the cup, celebrating, a tiny moment but one held forever on the TV that day.

Mum's not watching, never watches football now. I can't tell her I've seen him, but I've seen my dad. And he's like me, we've got the same arms, we've got the same wiry legs, we move the same way. I'm part of him and he's part of me. But I know nothing about him. My dad, I don't know my dad. I need to know. So back in the box I go.

He moves to the box containing his dad's memories. We see images of **John White** *through the years.*

Scene Five

1955. Musselburgh.

John   It's 1955 and I'm doing keepie uppies with an orange in our lobby and there's a knock on the door, I answer it. 'Is your brother home?' It's Jack 'Johnny' Love, Walsall manager but from Edinburgh. I know him but he clearly doesn't know me.

'Which brother?' I ask. 'The footballer.' 'Aye well all three of us play.' 'Your big brother, John White.' I'm a bit taken aback by this. 'I'm John White.' 'You?' 'Aye.' 'Oh.' 'Yeah.' 'Right well the thing is I'm Johnny Love.' 'I know who you are.' 'My coaching staff speak very highly of you.' 'Me?' 'They do aye. And we'd like to sign you for Walsall.' 'Right.' 'So. What do you think?' 'I'm earning good money as a joiner and playing for Bonnyrigg Rose.' 'What they paying you?' 'Five shillings a week from them but three pounds on top of that as a joiner.' 'We can double that.' 'The five shillings?' 'The pounds, the lot and you'll not be scraping by and playing football on the side, you'll be a professional footballer, John.' 'In England?' 'Unless Walsall's moved since I left.' 'My mum's out.' 'What?' 'My mum, this is all quite a lot to think about, my mum's out. I'll need to speak to her.' 'You'll need to speak to your mum?' 'Is that alright?' 'Er, yeah sure, John, you speak to your mum. I'll be in touch.'

But Johnny Love doesn't get in touch, I never hear from Johnny again. And I replay that conversation again. 'Is your brother home? Your big brother the footballer, the one who doesn't have to ask his mum if he can sign for a professional football club.' The one who's not too slight, too small, not good enough. Making the right decision every time. Because the wrong one, you never know it can be your last.

And the darkness kicks in again, as the days get shorter, nights get longer. But I pull myself back out the darkness, and I'm running and I'm training. Middlesbrough give me a trial and I score but again they say I'm *too small*. I get stuck out on the wing, out of harm's way. I'm not having that. So the training focuses on growing.

He whisks up a concoction of sherry, cod liver oil and eggs.

Cod liver oil, sherry and eggs, whisked up together and down in one. I wanna be sick but I swallow it down, keep it all inside and I grow. Rangers watch me, they don't want me. Three things stand out in their report. *Too slight, too small, not good enough.* But I carry on, whisking those eggs into the sherry into the cod liver oil and I swallow and I grow and Rangers don't want me again, but Alloa they see me.

Alloa, who are prepared to pay my five shillings travel each game on top of my wage so I can give my mum the full four pounds a week wage while I live off win bonuses, they see me. Alloa, who have to push kick-off forward fifteen minutes each week as we get into the darker months, because they can't afford floodlights. Alloa, who like me struggle so hard as those darker winter months set in desperate for winter to end, they see me, see what I can be. I turn eighteen and they sign me, not John White the part-time joiner. They sign John White the man, the footballer.

Scene Six

January 1974. Chelsea. **Rob White**, *still nine years old, is sat on the substitutes' bench at Stamford Bridge.*

Rob I'm on the bench, the Derby County bench at Stamford Bridge. I'm still nine years old, I'm not a sub, but Dad's old team mate Dave Mackay's been made manager of Derby, this is their first match in London and he's invited me along to the team hotel, the dressing room and now out onto to the pitch, well the bench.

See Mackay knows what being a leader is all about, it's not just being strong, it's not just being fierce although we're all probably familiar with the pic of him having Billy Bremner up by the throat. Dave Mackay knows that a leader is there and he knows my dad's not been there. Not through any fault of mine, not through any fault of my dad's. January means we've made it through another Christmas, Nat King Cole on the radio singing 'I feel so sorry for that laddy he hasn't got a daddy, the little boy who Santa Claus forgot'. I'm a footballer's son who grew up without a footballer in his life.

Except I didn't, not totally, that's what Dave Mackay's giving me today, he's giving me what my dad would have given me. I'm Scottish and he gives me a link to there and that Derby team . . . They give me the connection I need, the connection I'm missing, that thing a little Scottish boy misses out on being brought up in the suburbs by an English mum and nan. And I can't let my mum know that that's what I'm missing out on, because what can she do? She's doing her best, doing all she can so I can never tell her, but today's what I need. Men, adult men, smelly men, strong men. And Scots, Dave Mackay, but also today there's *Archie Gemmill*.

Archie Gemmill is my absolute hero, not the most gifted footballer in the world, not blessed with the most skill or looks but has that thing that's absolutely irresistible to any young boy growing up looking for a role model. Everything about Archie Gemmill screams 'Fuck it, I won't give in. I will succeed.'

Stood next to Archie Gemmill, so many things I want to say but I'm too scared. Dave introduces me to the squad. 'This is Rob, John White's son', and there's that look again. 'Such a tragedy, what a player your dad was.' That sad knowing look I get every time. That endless look of sympathy that's already stamped itself on my life.

But I'm not being that, not today, today I'm Archie Gemmill, today I'm that mantra 'Fuck it, I won't give in. I will succeed' and I'm heading out the tunnel and I'm sat on the bench and there's boys my age in the stand leaning over trying to get autographs trying to be as close, even for a second as close as I am to these men, this world of football.

The smell of the dressing room, Wintergreen, football's chosen brand of deep heat burns itself deep into my nostrils forever, the noise of studs on concrete, plaster tape being ripped around socks and just masculine noise. Like a foreign world to me until then. The low sound of men's voices, focussed. Not raucous. A controlled manly sound. Grown-up words, that language between men and I'm a boy, but today, today Dave Mackay's made me part of that world. As well as the physical genetics, there's something else we pass on. Something mental in our DNA, that connection, that world that Dad would have passed on to me but he couldn't, that's what Dave Mackay passed on to me that day. I'm part of my dad's world.

Scene Seven

1959. Scotland. National Service. **John White** *is running.*

John   You make decisions but life, or how far you get in life, falls into three key areas. Skill, hard work and luck. Skill will get you so far, skill might get you admired, but you think because you're born with ability you deserve success?

Skill with a fair amount of luck might get you quite a long way. Luck plays no small part, being in the right place at the right time. But hard work. Hard work is doing the right thing when nobody's watching. Working harder than lads who weren't brought up like you. Lads who've not had to walk out barefoot into the garden in the freezing cold to go to the toilet at night because you literally don't have a pot to piss in.

And that combination of skill and hard work has got me noticed. At Alloa, Rangers watch me again and again they decide, too small, too weak, not good enough. So I keep up, my skill it's always there and I work hard, I always work hard and even if Rangers don't see it, Hibs see it and Falkirk see it. And they start a bidding war to see who'll pay the most to sign John White. Like a poker game Hibs offer more, so Falkirk offer more and both clubs are fixed at three thousand three hundred pounds. So it's a draw but that's where luck comes into it, see the offers are the same but Falkirk's director runs a grocers and he says to Alloa, 'We'll give you three thousand three hundred pounds and a crate of whisky from my shop.' So Alloa take the whisky and I sign for Falkirk.

And my first game for Falkirk I score and we beat Celtic, then Scotland come knocking, I make my debut for them and in the first minute I score against West Germany. And I've done my country proud, but they come knocking again my country and they want me to represent them again, but it's not football this time, no. National Service, those Germans I scored against at Hampden are different to the ones we faced in war fourteen years earlier. But footballer or not to National Service I go.

So now I'm running. Not because anyone's watching, it's doing the right thing every time. Because if you do the right thing every time, then when the right person is watching then they see what you're made of. Now this (*references the run he is on*) *is* army cross-country running and the people

I'm running alongside they're not worried about skill, not worried about luck. Soldiers, pushing further, seeing the actual limits of what they can do.

Now I've commanded these men, had my own troop and I'm a bit naughty I guess. I've got them lined up the beach and I says 'run' so they say 'which way, sir?' And I'm naughty so I point at the sea. So they run and they don't stop running, through the paddling level, through the waves, past the point where your balls start to feel the cold, right up to their necks and that's when they turn and hear me laughing and see I've run off the other way. And they're calling me all sorts now but also they're good lads and see the funny side and they're laughing. But today nobody's laughing, because today we compete.

And there's three hundred men running through these fields and to start we're lined up alphabetically by surname, I'm right at the back, trying to make my way through but there's three hundred men and I'm having to trample my way past. Slow and steady? No, fast and steady and I make my way through that pack, I make my way past a hundred, two hundred men and now there's a hundred ahead of me now, but I'm fitter, I work harder. I. Won't. Stop.

National Service unavoidable but it doesn't exactly help your chances of playing for Scotland if you can't train with your teammates every day. And me being away with military doesn't help Falkirk either. They slide down, down, down the table. Last game of the season and we need to beat Raith to stay up but we're losing two-one and we're going down but there's a lifeline, the ref gives us a penalty but nobody wants to take it.

So I step up and I see Charlie Drummond in goal, Raith keeper but lives in Falkirk, he knows what football means to the town, doesn't want us to go down, hurt his own people. He looks at me, and he points right, I've seen it and he nods. He wants this to go in. And I just can't, I want us to stay up but I can't cheat. Charlie points again but I can't do it. I step up and smash it over the bar. Charlie looks at me confused. Falkirk are relegated. I need to move on.

And I make my way past another fifty now, but the ground's trudged up, but I won't be left behind, I won't stop and I make it past another ten, another twenty and there's thirty ahead of me here. And these men, training to be soldiers, not training to do keepie uppies, training because war's a recent pain and one we don't want to go through again. So the race is on now and I'm past one, two, three, four. I'm flying by them now as I motor on past.

But something else comes in my eye-line. NO. I overtake the lad who was in second place and my legs moving so much faster than the lad in first but I can see it and it's getting too close now. The finishing post, and he's too close, lad in first, and so I give it my last burst, but I can see the line and it's too near so I throw myself. Throw my body over the line and we both cross but he's ahead the other lad, by a smidge, by a nipple, but he's there first.

I'm broken on the floor, I've given everything, not because anyone's watching, this is for me. Because if you do the right thing every time. Try your absolute hardest every time. The skill and the luck don't need to matter. They take care of themselves.

Because later that day when Bill Nicholson, Spurs manager, has heard great things about me but worried physically I've not got what it takes, he calls my drill sergeant. The drill sergeant who's just watched that race, he says: 'Lacks stamina? Are you joking? Sign that boy.' So Bill decides to pay twenty thousand five hundred pounds and I sign for Tottenham Hotspur.

Scene Eight

25 January 1982. North London. **Rob White**, *now eighteen, is holding a box.*

Rob It's my eighteenth birthday and a very different box in front of me today from the one I've been dipping into all my childhood searching for my dad. I know what's inside this one. Eighteen today, another of those landmarks Dad missed out on.

I'm still living at home, studying for my A levels in the week and at weekends playing Sunday league football. Most of our matches are in Pymmes Park, Edmonton. The pitches might only be a mile or two from White Hart Lane where Dad played but believe me this is a different world. Since fifteen I've been playing in a men's league and I do not belong here. Not just the age gap that makes me feel alien, everywhere I go on the pitch I feel lost. I just want someone to tell me, kick it like that, run like this. I want my dad to tell me, not that I'm doing well, but offering guidance of some kind. Mum and Nan who I live with, they never came to my matches, not that having them on the sidelines telling me what to do would have done me any favours in an Edmonton pub league anyway.

Without a dad around it's understandable to some extent what happened. Living in the area we did there was always a chance there would be men like that nearby.

'Do you like playing football?' That voice, the voice of an older man, a neighbour, an older man who found me when I was just ten years old playing by myself. I was ten, playing football was my world, but looking up at this older man I didn't know what to say. I nodded. 'Why don't you come and train with us?' I know, I know who this man is, I run, I turn away and I run. That man, some of you will have heard of this man, Arsenal manager, Bertie Mee, if I hadn't run away that day, I know life is full of what-ifs but if I hadn't made that decision that day I could have ended up training with Arsenal. It just doesn't bear thinking about.

As a kid at school nobody ever spoke about who my dad was but they must have known because nobody ever asked. Divorce wasn't really an option back then, certainly not round where I grew up so if you went to a mate's house their mum and dad were there, a dad who's actually there not in a box, the box I carry everywhere I go. Not physically but mentally that weight is always there, sometimes like a shopping bag, a bearable weight but one you want to put down once you're home but you can't. Other days like a full fridge on your back, a double fridge freezer strapped to your back and you can't even take the slightest step because you know you haven't got the balance and it'll crush you so you just can't move.

But I'm eighteen now, I'm a man so I can't be thinking about that, because men don't, men just get on with things, keep it all wrapped up inside the box. Not the box I have in front of me here though.

Because this box in front of me I really don't need to open it I know what it is, my mates are sniggering and I know what they've dug out.

He opens the box.

That red Arsenal shirt I was given by Bertie Mee who tried to corrupt my childhood and a signed photo of their 1971 side, things I was given as a child and without a father there to protect me made their way into our family home. My friends laugh as I throw the shirt back in the box in disgust.

Back in the box they go. I'm eighteen today, I don't need a father's guidance now. But my search for him carries on, it never ended. I don't think it ever will.

Scene Nine

March 1960. White Hart Lane. **John White** *stands alone looking a bit annoyed.*

John   So I'm a bit pissed off to tell you the truth. National Service, two years I'm up and I'm down. London back to Scotland but now I'm done, demobbed as of today. And they drop me here, I'm not expecting a welcome home party you know, not expecting a victory parade but they drop me here at White Hart Lane but nobody knew I was coming.

I go into reception and she's confused. 'What are you doing here, John?' London is not my home. I don't mean in the way Musselburgh will always be my home, I mean I don't have a home in London. The months since signing for Spurs I've been up and down back to Scotland so much the club's put me up in digs. 'The landladies we use, they're all booked up,' she says. 'All of them?' 'The others are away for the bank holiday weekend. Are you sure you're not up in Scotland with the army?' 'Aye, I'm pretty sure I'm stood here right in front of you now am I not?' 'I know, sorry I mean. Well I don't really know what to do John.'

This is not the welcome home I'd been hoping for, the poor girl on the desk is obviously feeling a bit stressed with this and I know it's not her fault but. 'Well where are you going to stay?' says the girl and now I'm feeling stressed, I'm tired and there she is asking me the very question I'm meant to be asking her and I'm about to respond when: 'Now what's all this then?' A voice of calm, a voice I'm familiar with, a fatherly voice. Harry Evans, assistant manager, walks into reception. Harry's the man who believed in me when I stopped believing in myself, when Bill Nick signed me and I trained with this team and I said 'I'm not good enough to play with these players'. Harry believed in me and he's here now.

'It's John White,' says the girl. 'He's not up in Scotland with the army like we thought.' 'I can see that,' says Harry. 'Well the club have nowhere free you see, there's nowhere we can put him.' 'Now that's not true,' says Harry. 'We've nowhere, really Mr Evans, all the landladies are full or away.' 'He's coming to stay with me,' says Harry. 'Oh thank you so much,' says the girl on the desk, saying my thoughts out loud. Harry puts his arm around me. 'Got all you need?' he asks, I nod and follow him to his car with my wash stuff and little bag of clothes.

We get in Harry's car. 'You hungry?' he asks. 'Aye I could eat.' 'Good, Alma's making her famous steak and kidney pie.' We drive, get to his house, home. We step inside. 'We've another mouth to feed,' he says. Alma replies. 'I wish you'd tell me these things before . . .' She starts to tell Harry off but sees me. 'Sorry, dear, lovely to see you, John, plenty to eat, lovely to have you, go take a seat.'

I walk through to the lounge, I'm about to sit down when something happens. Something that changes the rest of my life. Decisions. You see I could have turned away and found a hotel, the second the girl on the desk at Spurs says there's no room at the inn I could have walked straight back out. And what happens then? Then Harry doesn't walk into reception. Then he doesn't put me up at his and offer Alma's pie, then this next moment doesn't happen.

Sandra walks into the lounge, Harry and Alma's girl, nineteen, beautiful, stunning but beyond that, something way beyond any girl I'd ever seen. Sandra walks in and maybe I'd got to use to the smell of eleven sweaty muddy men piling into my same bath, maybe it was having the best part of a year with nowhere to call home but Sandra walks in and suddenly life feels right.

'Anything you want?' Sandra asks. 'You?' I reply. 'What?' 'You, what are you having?' 'I'll probably have a sherry with my lunch.' A shout through from the kitchen. 'Oh will you now?' comes Alma's voice. 'Aye, that sounds good,' I say. 'Yes I will, Mum, me and John are having a sherry with our lunch.'

We move through and take a seat around the table, Alma dishes up. 'Lucky I made such a big one,' she says dolloping a healthy wedge of pie on my plate. I take a bite and 'Oh'. I don't think there's anything in the world I've tasted worse. As much as I've tried to acclimatise to London it's still a foreign city to me. My aunt Maggie's still sending me aspirins in the post because she thinks they're a Scottish thing you can't get down here and in terms of the food she's got a point. Now a pie in Scotland is something you can actually eat and enjoy but in England . . . Well it seems they have a different idea of what a pie is.

For as glad as I am to have a roof over my head I'm thinking now I'd rather be out in the streets than swallow another bite of whatever this is. I have to think, talk, you can't put food in your mouth while you're talking so I get the conversation going.

'You one of the people who believe we can do the double, Sandra?' I figure that'll get the chat going. 'It's more if *you* believe it that's the issue isn't it, John? Bill and Dad are good enough so it's a case of whether you can get over yourselves and do the job,' says Sandra. Silence

God I love Sandra already, most girls talking to a footballer would be a highlight, not for her, I guess with who her dad is she's grown up used to it. That or I make so little impression on girls they don't care if they offend me or not. 'Right,' I say, back to silence and Alma's pie, which if anything looks as though it's grown.

My attempt at sparkling conversation's fallen short and the fire behind me has me sweating. I'm going to have to take another bite of this. 'Oh I've left the oven on,' Alma says and darts out to the kitchen and this is my chance. Alma goes to the kitchen and Harry turns his head as she goes, I fling the remains of my pie on the fire. Sandra sees this and gives me a wicked smile but says nothing. I tuck into the rest of my lunch.

We all finish and Alma's offering me seconds. 'I couldn't, honestly,' I say. 'OK then, the speed at which you put that away I can tell you liked it, I'll be sure to make it again next time.' I smile and say nothing, Sandra catches my eye and I try not to laugh. I go to sit in the lounge. 'Where do you think you're going?' says Harry. 'Sorry, Harry, I thought I was OK to stay?' 'You are, lad, but the girls made the lunch so we're washing up.'

I've never actually washed a dish before, I'm in the kitchen stood with Harry and I can see he's wanting to laugh but he doesn't, again he puts a kind hand on my arm. 'Your mum always take care of this kind of thing?' 'Aye well Dad, well he . . .' 'I know,' says Harry. 'I'm not sure even if he'd been around he'd have . . .' 'Yeah well in this house men pull their weight.' Harry shows me, we wash the dishes, then we wipe the dishes dry, we don't speak. This just feels, I don't know, right I guess. We finish. 'Off you go then,' says Harry, 'make yourself at home.'

I do. By the time I move out Sandra and me are married.

Scene Ten

20 July 1996. North London. **Rob White** *is on crutches and holding two wedding rings.*

Rob   London during the summer of 1996, often regarded as the best ever time to be a football fan. Everybody coming together in one hot amazing summer culminating in my wedding. Perfect right? Unless of course you happen to, by virtue of my father, be a Scot living in London. Forced to endure endless highlights of England's win over Scotland.

In an attempt to distract from the endless repeats of McAllister's penalty miss followed swiftly by Gazza's goal I decide to step out onto the pitch myself, not Wembley but Market Road astroturf. I'm brought in on the sly to play for a mate's team. Weekend before my wedding, this should prove the perfect distraction from seating plans and discussing bunting.

No seat needed for my dad obviously but even the date casts his shadow over the day. Married 20th July, the day before my father was killed. A new date of hope and joy, the day before one which will forever hold such sad memories.

If playing a football match was supposed to be a nice distraction from wedding plans I was soon brought crashing back to earth in the shape of a tackle which even when Dad was playing would have been considered pretty fucking shocking. There's only one way you can dislocate your ankle, a precise point of contact snapping the tendon leaving your foot flapping around in your sock.

Ambulance to the Whittington Hospital speeds by my house on Bickerton Road where shortly a teammate, who's had to drive my car home for me, will inform my fiancée that I won't exactly be *walking* up the aisle. At the hospital the doctor explains he can either leave the ankle as it is until the operation or snap it back into place. Snapping the ankle back into the joint bringing the foot and leg back together is better in the long run but will be incredibly painful.

As someone just about to get married I can hardly ask for the less painful option of letting the two remain separated can I? So I grit my teeth, the way I've had to all summer watching Scotland's demise in Euro '96, and the doctor snaps the leg back in place.

Which brings me here today. Two rings like this, a wedding day and two rings come together, bring two people together in marriage. Two rings brought together like this.

He pushes the two rings together and now they're forged together.

These were Dad's rings, the ones he was wearing when he died, forged together, forged together in this unending symbol of infinity somehow. They think he must have had his hands clasped together like this when lightning struck.

He clasps his hands.

And the rings forged. Brought together and making a symbol, this symbol, the number eight, Dad's number.

He places the forged rings and his dad's old shirt in the box.

I don't miss Dad on my wedding day. How can you mourn someone you never knew? But as much as I didn't want to dislocate my ankle I always have this niggling thought that

in a way it was me trying to avoid getting married somehow.
Dad wasn't able to show me how to be a husband, how would
I know what to do?

After Mum and Dad's wedding at the hotel, the band played
'MacNamara's Band', the song Spurs would come out to,
everyone in the hotel look at them and he blushed bright
red. He could play in front of sixty thousand people but
without a ball he could't bear the limelight, something I've
clearly inherited from him.

Pushing all shyness aside I hobble my way up the aisle and
start a new stage in life, not just a son to a dead father, not
just a man in my own right, a husband. Two forged together
as one, for as long as it lasts. Because how long does
anything really last?

Scene Eleven

January 1963. North London. Hospital, **John White** *in extreme
pain.*

John   Hospital. I just want something to take away this
pain. Waiting for the doctor and trying to distract my mind
from the agony in my back. Nobody likes hospitals do they?
Only happy time was when Sandra was in giving birth to our
girl Mandy. Aye we're a family now. That awful pie washed
down with a sherry. That sherry led to more sherries and
suddenly we're having a little girl. I had to do the right thing
this time. We married just in time so she's born honest.

I buy Sandra a new coat as a wedding present, Bill Nick sees
it. 'Get that thing off, no red at White Hart Lane.' 'I'll buy
you another,' I tell her and I do, but by the time I get round
to it that same day she goes into labour and before I know it
I'm bringing home Sandra from hospital with our girl.
Harry and Alma waiting at home for our victorious return.
Harry's smile, one I'll never see again. Flash in a pain. Think
of something else.

17th April 1961 me and Harry still living under the same roof. It's three o'clock in the morning but neither of us can sleep. 'Whisky?' says Harry. 'We've got Sheffield Wednesday tomorrow, well tonight.' 'I know,' says Harry, pouring two large glasses, and finally I sleep.

And that night we play but I'm tired and we go behind, but I find the strength. We do it that night, we come from behind and Spurs beat Sheffield Wednesday and Spurs are champions of England but that's only half the job done.

Nineteen more days until the FA Cup Final. Nineteen more days and Spurs are at Wembley and every decision I made proves right, because Spurs go out and beat Leicester and we're the first side in the twentieth century to do the double. But even the double's not enough, not for Bill Nick, he thinks we could have played better, but at home Harry's happy. But then Harry starts to get sick.

Happy memories of hospitals long gone now. My pain's that bad I can't sleep, not a wink. Club doctor's told me it's psychosomatic, that I should rest, but I can't rest. Can't rest if you can't sleep and I can't sleep because the pain's that bad.

There's a nurse talking to Sandra. 'He's been like this since my dad died,' she says. 'What's that got to do with anything? I might not be a doctor, but I know Harry's cancer is not the reason my back can't move.'

Doctor arrives, Sandra speaks. 'There's a lot going on. I think he needs to talk to someone.' 'I don't need to talk, talking's not gonna fix my back.' The doctor smiles. 'Has anything someone said helped coping with things?' 'I can cope perfectly well.' 'Your manager?' 'Bill? You want me to go to him and say my head's not right?' 'Whatever this is, it's affecting your football too right?' 'Danny understands. Our skipper, when these dark months come he says recognise when you're having a bad day and take less risks.' 'Does that help?' 'For a bit. Can I have something for the pain?' 'This should help you sleep'

And I drink it, but I don't sleep. I talk, to the doctor or to the walls. I wanna talk to Harry but like Dad he's gone, left me, left Sandra, cancer took him on Alma's birthday, left his wife a birthday card the day he died with two words inside: 'Sorry, mate.' I talk and I hear my words.

Winter comes and the light goes away as it always does. And I run but I can't run like I usually do and I pass a ball but it doesn't spin the way it should do. And I know it's coming, every year the same. But if anything knowing it's coming makes it worse. So I work harder, train harder, but the darkness is getting earlier and earlier as the days get shorter. Energy, sapped. Confidence, drained. And this weight builds up you can't run a mile carrying a weight like that let alone the ten I run every day.

And at home she can't understand but that weight is all I have to give and I can't give her that. So I carry it, cos I love her. Bury it deep inside, but I'll be back soon.

Scene Twelve

2002. Musselburgh. Janette White's sixtieth. We hear the pulse of a beat as Sister Sledge plays and the spinning of lights gives us the feel that a group of people are dancing. **Rob White** *is called over by his uncle, unseen, and dances a little.*

Rob   'Ha. That right, Tom? To be honest I'd say you're a better footballer than you are dancer.' It's my aunt Janette's sixtieth so I'm back in Musselburgh. I say back, I've never lived here but so much family here this will always be a part of me. A part of my home. Dad never being able to bring me here's made it more so if anything.

So we've all had a drink and if there's one thing I'm trying to avoid more than dancing to Sister Sledge it's my uncle Tom. Basically every family event like this while my aunt's singing

'We Are Family' at the top of her voice, he gets pissed and goes on at me about what a crap uncle he's been. I mean I don't know what an uncle is supposed to be but he's been OK as far as I can tell but get a few drinks in him and he corners me every time and goes on about how shit he's been. It's annoying to be honest. I've asked a few of the family to not leave me alone with him and that's worked so far but this song's come on and he's cornered me.

'I've been a crap uncle.' 'I'm fine, Tom.' 'I have been.' 'Yeah well . . . I'm getting a drink.' 'Wait.' 'What?' 'I have, I've been a terrible uncle.' 'Why do you always say this?' 'Not just to you.' 'Mandy's got no problem with you.' 'The other one, the wee lad.' 'I think you've had a few too many, Tom. You do know Mandy's a girl right? Well a woman?' 'There was another.' 'What?' 'Before. John, he had a son.' 'Mum never said.' 'Not with your mother, up here. John was just a lad himself.'

This catches me like a punch to the stomach, everything inside flips one way while my head goes the other.

'What?' 'Local mantrap. Your dad got had. He did the right thing by her, he sent money, he didn't blame her, he did the right thing.' 'I've got a half-brother?' 'John behaved impeccably, you have to know that. I didn't want you thinking less of your dad. It was her, the girl.' 'I don't think it works that way, Tom. What did she tie his laces together and he fell into bed with her?' 'I've been a crap uncle.' 'Why are you telling me this?' 'Because you're a man now, you deserve to know.'

And as much as I can see why Tom didn't want to tell me I'm glad I know. And as much as he didn't want me to think less of my dad it's good to know that Dad was real. Not some perfect ghost kept upstairs in a box wrapped up in tissue paper. A man, not whiter than white. A man who fucked up sometimes, yeah he was one of the best footballers who ever lived but he made mistakes. Made decisions he had to live with. Had a kid he never saw, a secret. Well not a secret from

everyone, Mum knew, she sent the cheques every week a
payment went up. I guess Mum didn't trust Dad to
remember so she sent the money each week. Not a perfect
man, but a man, a human man.

Scene Thirteen

October 1962. North London. **John White** *is locked out of his
house.*

John   'Sandra. Sandra it's John, open up the door.' She's
only gone and done it, said she would. 'If you're not back by
eleven I'm putting the bolt on.' It's like five past eleven, well
not long gone eleven. Well it wasn't long gone eleven when I
left the Bell and Hare. The drive home took a while but
what's she want me to do? I don't like to drive fast if I'm
pissed you know, safety first.

I didn't even wanna go out really, but I mean if Dave Mackay
says you're going for a drink what you gonna do you know?
I guess it's my decision but . . . Then once we're out
everyone's there, the players of course and few local
characters, the gangster One Armed Lou, ticket tout, mates
with the Krays but a good laugh. So we're drinking and Cliff
Jones is there and . . . well you know how it is. Before you
know it we've nicked an ice cream bike and we're driving it
around selling ice creams to all the lads. We gave the ice
cream fella back the money for what we sold.

Anyway it's turned into a bit of a night, but what's she want
me to do, sleep out here? I love her, I love her more than
anything in the world but I don't wanna freeze to death. (*He
gets an idea.*) I know.

He nips around the back of the house.

That's the handy thing see of having a skill, a trade before
football. That skill as a joiner's come in useful. Just chip the
putty out of this here back window.

He attempts to chip away the window putty.

For a time even with being married and having the baby we were still living at Harry's. Spurs get us a place but Sandra reckons it smells funny so we get this house here, Church Street. Bit of a state but me having been a joiner I can do it up myself. See nothing around the house I can't do.

He attempts to chip the last bit of putty away. We hear the window break.

Ah anyway I'm in now. I'll sleep it off. Need to be fresh tomorrow, big day tomorrow and it comes.

We hear the sound of a radio and the Cup Winners' Cup drawer. He strips into his kit.

Draw for the second round of the European Cup Winners' Cup, there's sixteen teams in the hat, fifteen possible opponents. Fifteen ways this could turn out, but I know which way this is gonna go. Before they've even made the drawer, this is fate, I know who we're getting. Tottenham Hotspur of England will be facing . . . Glasgow Rangers of Scotland. Rangers who said I was too slight. Rangers who said I was too small. Rangers will be coming to White Hart Lane. Rangers who said I'd never be good enough. And Spurs will be going to Ibrox. Rangers who had me watched forty times. Forty times I had those eyes burning into the back of my head, with every run, with every touch, every decision I made they analysed. And forty times they decided the same, he's too slight, too small, not good enough. Aye well we'll see about that won't we?

He takes the field.

Bill Nick sends us out, he's analysed them, had them watched, tells us what we need to do. Not a word goes in, I know what I have to do. My pre-match talk is every word one of their scouts, one of their coaching staff, one of their managers has said about me over the years, in their reports, in their chats, over drinks in the pub. Every one of them that said I'd never make it at the top, that's what I'm hearing as we take the field. Danny's saying something about how good we are, I don't need that either today. Today's about John White and the forty times Rangers watched him in the past and the time they actually came up against him.

Kick-off and we're on fire that night, we batter them from the first whistle, more skill, more pace and physically aye we can mix it as well. Rangers cannot live with us. For three minutes they weather the storm but fourth minute from a corner the ball comes to me. I don't even think, I don't need to make a decision, the net's bulging and I'm running off celebrating. Four minutes gone and John White puts Spurs ahead against Glasgow Rangers. Four minutes it took me to show them what they missed out on forty times. But I'm not done yet, twenty-three minutes and I've done it again. Too slight, too small, not good enough. I've scored again and I keep going we keep going. Spurs five Rangers two.

Is that good enough Rangers? Is that good enough for you? Whatever Rangers think of it, it's certainly not good enough for Bill Nick, in the dressing room he's letting us know we've not done enough and even to the press. 'I'm really not pleased, we can play a lot better'. I go to bed with that ringing in my ears.

But it's not rest, this isn't normal sleep, a normal sleep you can wake up from, a normal sleep I'm back up in the morning and running ten miles, twenty. This isn't tiredness, those cold dark winter months set in again and I can't move let alone run, I can't get out of bed. December starts but I'm nowhere to be seen.

Spurs play out a dour nil–nil that weekend but I'm still in my bed. 'I've got flu,' I say, I need to rest, so I stay in my bed because that week, I know what's coming up, that week we go to Rangers and Bill Nick's right, as great as we played 5–2 is not enough up there, Glasgow crowd at Ibrox, concede an early goal up there and they'll be on us. Not one person watching you forty times, eighty thousand Glasgow Rangers fans watching you once seeing that every scout every coach every manager was right. John White's not good enough.

Monday I'm still in my bed and the club doctor comes to the house. 'You're fine.' 'I'm full of flu, doc.' 'You're fine, the train to Glasgow's tomorrow, you're fit to travel, we expect you on it.' But Tuesday comes and I'm not on that train, I've not left my bed and Spurs head to Scotland without John White.

And my head's just full, not just cold and snot, a cloud a heavy fog comes down and lands just right on my brain and it spreads and the Spurs train is delayed with this fog, the driver can't see fifty feet in front of him so he has to crawl the train into Glasgow at four miles an hour. But still this fog spreads and it sits and it fills the park at Ibrox and the referee steps out on the pitch and he's eaten by this fog. 'The pitch is fine,' Scot Symon, Rangers manager, says. 'I can't see either goal,' says the ref. 'I'm calling it off'.

And Spurs head back to London, the game will be rearranged, when the fog's gone, when it's clear. So December carries on and I'm still in my bed and Spurs lose away at Bolton. THEN IT CLEARS. I'm out my bed I'm bright, I'm back on the training ground. I'm John White. And we head to Scotland, Spurs head straight to Glasgow but not me, I stop in at Alloa, see my old pals, I see the old kit man. 'What's gonna happen tomorrow?' 'I'm gonna fucking stuff them.'

And it's Rangers v Spurs. Rangers who watched me forty times versus John White. Ibrox Park packed and full of the belief they never had in me, belief that they can turn this round. Kick-off and we need to shut this lot up quick but they just won't go quiet. Jimmy Greaves puts us ahead and they're still making a racket. Second half and Rangers equalise, we're still three up on the tie but they just will not shut up, we go ahead again but they're still singing and they equalise again, two-all on the night. We'll go through but that's not enough, those that said John White's not good enough will feel vindicated. I couldn't do it at the top level, at Ibrox in front of eighty thousand I wasn't enough.

No. Fucking. Way. I pick the ball up on the left, three of their lads around me trying to kick lumps out of me but they can't get near. Me in all white, our European all-white strip, even in all that mud you can't miss me but I disappear from each of them. Papers have started calling me 'the ghost' and I prove why here. Disappear from every kick and tackle they try to land on me and I spin past the three and I put a ball in, land it on Bobby Smith's head, a perfect cross I literally could not have landed it on him better, he cannot miss, but he does, well he heads it but the mud's stopped it before it's crossed the line but he's followed it in and it's in the back of the net and I've made the winner. I've destroyed Rangers again. And now they're quiet and now I can rest.

Scene Fourteen

5 November 2006. **Rob White** *is standing in the tunnel at White Hart Lane.*

Rob 'Go away, Ashley.' The firm authoritative voice of the referee. I'm stood in the tunnel at White Hart Lane about to step out on the pitch. Again the opponents are Chelsea and again I'm not playing, or a sub, I'm not heading out with my teammates, instead stood beside me are two little girls, my daughters Elsie and Martha. I'm nervous myself, the thought of stepping out in front of thirty-six thousand people filling me with fear, but at the moment that has to be pushed aside, back in the box. Because at the moment I need to be a father and protect my daughters.

We hear beeping sounds we are familiar with from television, used to bleep out obscenities.

Is the response from Ashley Cole of Chelsea who is hiding in a secluded corner of the tunnel in order to shout things at the referee.

My daughters aren't too familiar with this language but the referee is. 'I've got nothing to say to you, Ashley, now get in your dressing room'. I look at Elsie and Martha, the look on their faces show they know these are naughty words.

We're about to step out. Dad's being inducted into the Spurs hall of fame and the club have asked me to come out at half-time and receive a decanter with his name engraved, I've said yes on the proviso that the girls can come too. A nice decanter I can fill with wine, I can fill with spirits, that can be used, not locked away somewhere like Dad's old things.

That box is empty now, things aren't all stashed away in tissue paper up in an attic like a ghost, they're either lost to time or hung with pride somewhere. A complete account of my search for my father would take a lifetime to tell because that's how long I've been looking.

The trouble was that nobody at home ever talked about Dad, no pictures on the wall. Just me and my sister's faces a constant reminder to my mum of what she'd lost. The only thing I know for certain about Dad is what he smelt like, his old razor was passed onto me when he died and along with it a distinctive smell, one that as a boy I clung onto as the smell of Dad. As I got older I also learnt that the smell was actually Old Spice. One of Dad's teammates, Peter Baker, had the same smell and I checked the bottle.

This new bottle now, the decanter we'll be getting. Stepping out on the pitch, me, Elsie and Martha. I'd anticipated the fear, the emotion of being out on that turf that Dad had stepped out on so many times. What I hadn't anticipated were the cheers, for Dad, for us on Dad's behalf.

The Park Lane where I've sat for so long, united in cheering one of their greats. The blokes I've been sat next to for years also about to get a big surprise. Before our last game the bloke I've sat next to for the last decade has said, 'See you next week'. I've given the cryptic response, 'You'll see me but I won't see you'. Seeing me and the girls step out on the pitch I guess it'll make sense to him now. All those years, all those emotions we've been through together, there never seems an appropriate time to say, by the way my dad used to play for Spurs.

But cutting through that, before any of that what I hear is 'Ref you're a f(*bleep*)ing c(*bleep*)'. Now you've not heard that, but Elsie and Martha they've heard that and Clive Allen, our coach, his dad played with mine, he's heard that. 'Did you hear that, ref?' he says. 'He's not a bright lad is he, Clive?' replies the ref.

I take Elsie and Martha by the hand, I'm there for them. I feel so small, thirty-six thousand people and I feel like I could just disappear, but we're up there on the big screen. We go out on the pitch, get that decanter etched in our family name, Dad's name. Spurs win as well, that always helps. The crowd cheer our family name.

Scene Fifteen

21 July 1964. Crews Hill golf course, North London. **John White** *is preparing for a game of golf.*

John   'Three balls please.' Three new balls from the club shop. Three different balls, three different choices. Three different decisions, of the thousand decisions I made that day to get me here. Of the ten million decisions I made in life that got me to the one place I am now.

Three balls from the tee and any of the three I can follow, one slices to the right, one slices to the left slightly, but one I catch perfectly, one heads straight onto the fairway. And that's the way I'm going, that's the ball I follow, that's the decision I make. I follow along the fairway, on my own, just me and the ball I'm following. The sky turns grey but I'm following on.

Every moment of that day. Flashing before my eyes as the skies darken. Not heading straight to golf from training, stop off at home and get a new pair of trousers. Sandra's there. 'Where are your trousers?' 'One of the lads must have taken them.' 'Is that right?' 'What you think I'm off shagging at ten o'clock in the morning?' 'Where you going now?' 'Golf.' 'No you're not.' 'I'll not be long, nine holes.' 'You're staying here, the baby's had me up all night. You watch him and Mandy, I'm going to bed.' 'When I'm back.' 'Who you playing with?' 'Some of the lads.' 'You're not having the car.' 'What?' 'You're not having the car.' 'If I walk it'll be midnight before I'm back.' 'I'll drive you.' 'What?' 'I'll drive you, if you're just playing golf, a quick round, I'll drop you off, pick you up when you're done.' 'Why do you need the car?' 'I'll take the kids to Linda Baker's.' 'I thought you wanted a rest?' 'I want some adult conversation.' 'Fine.'

Sandra drops me here. Tony Marchi's in the locker room, he's on his own and I could ask him to stay and play a round with me, but he's got a right strop on cos he's been left out the team photo this morning, that's why he's been down here early. Left out that photo means he's not part of Bill Nick's plans. That's the manager's decision, but a lot can change. Even by the end of today there could be a slot in the side to fill. Anyway Tony's got this right grump on so I'd rather play on my own than listen to him go on. 'I'm just meeting some friends, Tony,' I say and head off to the club shop.

And I'm following my ball, with each step the sky turns darker. Each step another part of my journey. Too small as a baby, won't make it, won't survive, but I do, I grow as a kid footballer stuck out on the wing, but I prove myself, I make it at Bonnyrigg Rose, Alloa, Falkirk, Scotland, Tottenham Hotspur. I take another step and there's nothing light in the sky now, not even the clouds are white. The rain comes down but I take another swing and follow the ball. I reach my ball, the one of the three I've chosen and again three choices in front of me. I can head back into the clubhouse, grab a cheeky pint and wait for Sandra to pick me up, I can stay where I am and keep playing. Or I can grab shelter under that there tree.

He moves towards the tree he indicated.

And of the ten million decisions I make in life that's the final one.

Sudden blackout, flash of light, back to black.

Newspaper headlines: 'Spurs star killed by lightning'.

Scene Sixteen

21 July 2024. Tottenham, North London. **Rob White**, *now sixty, is at home stood beside hundreds of letters stacked around his father's leather case which he opened at the start.*

Rob   The loss that I carry is always with me and I carry it everywhere I go. From opening that box when I was eight to looking for his ashes as a middle-aged man, the thing I'm actually looking for is well gone. Like the lightning strike that killed him. You can try and bring the past back to life but it's not really real, however hard you try. I've learnt you can't keep things bottled up inside. Because like a feather pillow the second there's the slightest hole they spill out everywhere and you can't get them back in the case.

He turns to his father's leather case.

This case though, this one you *can* keep things inside, although I'm getting them out today. Hundreds of letters Mum got when Dad died, from Spurs, from the Scottish FA, from football clubs around the world, from kids. I'll never be able to make sense of my dad's death but even today I meet people who say the first time they saw their dad cry, or the only time they saw their dad cry was when they heard John White had died, football's always been this odd gateway drug I guess where blokes are actually allowed to expose emotion. Mum never said, but it must have helped, to some extent the letters must have helped, knowing that so many people out there cared.

He searches for a letter.

Bobby Collins, Scotland international, played with my dad. Letter from his wife to Mum: 'All footballers' wives will be thinking of you today'. These must have helped, just knowing that there's someone out there that has some idea of what you're going through, that even if they can't fully understand, they care and want to show they care.

I moved to this house a few years back. Spurs were founded in 1882 and this house is eighteen hundred and eighty-two feet from the new Spurs stadium. Eighteen hundred and eighty-two feet from the lamppost Spurs put up last year, it's to replicate the one a group of boys stood next to in 1882 when they decided that Tottenham needed a football club as they only played cricket at the time. Nobody's exactly sure where that lamppost was but I like the spot they chose because it's also equidistant between my house and White Cottage, Spurs' first official address.

I went to Crews Hill golf course. I'd been there once before but as a five-month-old sat in the car as Mum was being told there'd been a horrible accident. Today I get out the car. I don't know what I was expecting to find, answers? See the tree where it happened? Put my mind at rest maybe? I was worried, worried that where he'd breathed his last breath was now squalid, overgrown, abandoned or like some horrid *Crimewatch* reconstruction. It's not, I'm glad it's not. No answers no sign.

Then a sign does come, or it's someone up in the clouds with a dark sense of humour. I play a round of golf on my own, Gullane in Scotland. 'I'm not a member.' 'That's fine. Just you on your own?' 'Just me.' 'Right OK we'll need a contact number for next of kin.' 'Why?' 'Just in case there's some kind of emergency. Like you were struck by lightning say.' I stare incredulous for a second. There's nothing I can say to that.

It's sixty years on and Dad's long gone, the ghost, someone I never knew. Dad's gone but I know as much as I can about him, about as much as you can know about someone you never actually knew. Dad's not in that box, he's not up there in a cloud somewhere, he's everywhere even if you can't see him, just like he was on the pitch.

Scene Seventeen

15 May 1963. Rotterdam.

John Rangers couldn't stop us, couldn't stop me. Slovan Bratislava the same, OFK Beograd the same and Spurs are in a European final. Spurs can become the first British side to win a European trophy, but who is it we're up against? Atlético Madrid. Atlético the current holders, Atlético who have already won a European competition the previous year. Atlético who are big enough, strong enough, good enough, and Spurs? Well we'll have to wait and see.

We arrive out in Holland and nothing's left to chance, we've travelled with everything. No decisions left in our hands. The food we eat, chosen for us, not our decision. Made for us, prepared for us by English chefs, our chefs. The water we drink's the water we flew out with us. Nothing left to chance.

Dressing room and Bill Nick's going through each of the Atlético Madrid side in detail, how big they are, how strong they are, how good they are. How they've won a European trophy before because of how good they are. I'm starting to think their lads are twelve feet tall, bogey men. But Danny pipes in: 'Hang on, Bill, they haven't got me. They haven't got Jimmy Greaves, They haven't got Terry Dyson. They haven't got Cliff Jones. They haven't got John White, and with that we step out onto the pitch and we see them, they're not twelve feet tall, but we are.

Kick-off but we've won it before we've won the toss. Danny's won it for us, he's let us know who we are. Fuck whatever Atlético have done in the past, we're the only English side this century to have done the double and we'll be the first English side to win a European trophy. Before we've kicked a ball Danny's words have won it for us. Before Jimmy Greaves puts us ahead after a quarter of an hour we know what we are. So on thirty-five minutes when the ball's pulled back to me on the edge of the box, I didn't have to make a decision. The ball's in the back of the net, I've smashed it into the back of the net from outside the box in a cup final. Like I'm watching myself, like I'm doing the Kenneth Wolstenholme commentary myself watching me smashing it home. Watching myself from the outside now as Spurs beat Atlético Madrid five-one.

I've got my medal, me and Cliff celebrating with the fans. Danny's running along with the trophy and he passes it to me and I'm lifting it over my head. I'm big enough, I'm strong enough. I'm good enough. I'm looking at my medal and I don't want this moment to ever end. Nothing could get better than this.

But the moment does end in a flash, it's gone, the moment not the medal though, the medal's still on and I'm back in the hotel room with Sandra. 'I scored,' I says. 'I know,' says Sandra smiling. 'I scored.' 'I know, John. Look I didn't want to distract you but I was sick this morning.' 'You didn't drink the water did you? Club have provided everything.' 'No, John, I haven't drunk the water. I've been sick last few mornings, same as I was before Mandy.' 'What?' 'So I checked in with the club doctor. I didn't wanna distract you before the game but . . .' 'Are you . . .?' 'Yes, John.' 'We're having another baby?' 'Yes, John. We're going to have a son.'

Ends.